Southern
Messenger
Poets

DAVE SMITH, EDITOR

Pharaoh,
Pharaoh

Pharaoh, Pharaoh

POEMS

CLAUDIA EMERSON ANDREWS

Louisiana State University Press

Baton Rouge and London

1997

Designer: Laura Roubique Gleason
Typeface: Bembo
Printer and binder: Thomson-Shore, Inc.

Library of Congress Cataloging-in-Publication Data
Andrews, Claudia Emerson, 1957–
   Pharaoh, pharaoh : poems / by Claudia Emerson Andrews.
      p.   cm. — (Southern messenger poets)
   ISBN 0-8071-2158-4 (cloth : alk. paper). — ISBN 0-8071-2159-2
(paper : alk. paper)
   I. Title. II. Series.
PS3551.N4155P48   1997
811'.54—dc21   97-7077
                                                                         CIP

Grateful acknowledgment is made to the following periodicals, in which
some of the poems herein originally appeared: *America:* "Going Once, Going
Twice"; *Chattahoochee Review:* "Inheritance," "Timepiece"; *Crazyhorse:* "Barn
Cat," "Cleaning the Graves," "Phoenix," "Stoic"; *Five Points:* "First Tooth";
The Louisville Review: "Morphine Dreams"; *Ploughshares:* "Bait Man"; *Shenan-
doah:* "Bait," "The Milk Cow Speaks of Winter," "Plagues"; *Southern Human-
ities Review:* "Gossip"; *Southern Poetry Review:* "Prodigal," "Stable"; *Southern
Review:* "Auction," "Fortune," "Hawk," "Looking for Grandmother's Grave,"
"One Hand on the Wheel," "Skin Deep," "Transgressions"; *TriQuarterly:*
"Abandoned Farm Grave," "The Moon Is Made," "Romantic Fever," "The
Taxidermist."

For Jesse

Everything we cannot see is here.

—Robert Watson

CONTENTS

III

IV

Pharaoh,
Pharaoh

SEARCHING THE TITLE

I. In the courthouse

My interest in it is curiosity.
It was a generation lost before
my conception. Still, I am close enough
to feel cheated of it; the bitterness
I did inherit with clear title. The loss
begins with what I know, the land's legal
declension from *father, father's* to neighbors' names,
strangers' names, the names of corporations—
a place encumbered, unencumbered, zoned,
divided, fenced against what had been itself.

II. The map

The map unscrolls to an old, forgotten dimension.
I see its maker drew a fine compass,
ornate; *North, South, Orient, Levant* fade
before me, fail me. I am lost. And still
I see here what I can, imagine I,
one of its ghosts, wander this displaced
landscape. Yes, here the world is flat, bound where
the river waves its drawn, pale water, where
the pines stand mute, tedious. And here, the gaping
space the maker labeled the Indian Fields—

a void in the middle of all detail, whose acreage
the legend could tell me, exactly, in hundreds—lies
close, whole, beneath the span of one splayed hand,
the palm down that waved itself before me,
before I could command it, limit it,
reduce it to *my*, before it would be read
in its detail: heartline, lifeline, line
of fate, of fortune, the mounts of Jupiter
and Luna; the plain of Mars—cool, dry—lies
against what was grass and wind in grass.

III. The legend

The map's legend reminds me of another,
though both reveal the degree to which any truth
can be abstracted. A changeless place,
uncharted, lies beneath these fields—a cave
whose mouth is lost. The old folks used to sigh
and claim it breathed, exhaled one cool breath for days
before it needed another. They said
it knew no season, was only itself—
fixed—a finished darkness that had known fire
before their fire had ever been conceived.

A pineknot hisses, fumes, is swallowed up.
The smallest flame waves massive shadows here,
writhes against this version of the world
where bats with winged hands wring from its darkness
flight, cling to what we fear. Like theirs, my voice
comes back to me, but mine the voice of a stranger
I know I cannot trust. I discover
a cache of quartz confuses light like water.
And then, not painted, but relieved in ocher,
their hands appear before me, dance and wave;

familiar, they calm the darkness in this
deeper cradle, their palms smooth, blank stone.
The way back is lost to dream. I scroll
the map, turn my back on what cannot be mine,
even in memory. What I know, I own:
a murder of crows rises from a broken field
as though from violent seed; a blood-beech seethes
all winter; two hawks spar against the dusk-
marred pines. I don't dispute with them this boundary,
their shared desire for this sky, this spiraled lie:
and so to the point and place of beginning.

I

AUCTION

Some things bring nothing. Later there will be
a bonfire of palm-worn plow handles.
But a doll, pallid—china hands fractured—
brings fifteen dollars.
                    His bed they have hauled
out, the covers still on it, an old man's
nest of tangled flannel. I think he has
no daughters to know what must not be
sold. His late wife's dressing table gives up
its confused vanities: snaggletooth combs,
the warbled wire of hairpins, a lipstick,
a faint layer of blush over all. The sun-
shocked mirror denies this face, waves my hair,
widens my eyes, until I cannot see
the resemblance. Is this how she saw
herself? And over her shoulder the fields,
falling away from the house, steep with
distortion? Under her crushed narcissus,
the varicose wake of a mole heaves
as if the vagrant dead—grown bolder—rise,
thick palms bared for this shallow, movable darkness.

CLEANING THE GRAVES

The once a year we come here is as close
as my mother comes to mourning. These graves
are all she has left of land she hated
losing. And I am descended from this
loss: her mother, a woman who trapped
snowbirds for potpie, who let hens nest
in the kitchen in freezing weather
so they would lay better, who could wring their heads
from their bodies in one motion, who could
wrestle down a calf. "Your blood is that cold,"
she tells me, "but you don't know it yet, never
had hard times. Hard times could never kill one
of us." The old lie. I know she will always
see her mother in that hated cotton coat,
walking four deep white miles to work.
A figure never diminishing from sight,
that mother won't succumb to something so
gentle as decay. Not ashes, not dust—
never was and won't be, and neither will
mine; her blood is that cold.
                                  Still, all my life
I have asked after her happiness
as if it were closer kin. I watch her
wrestle away from the grave the fallen
white rib of a sycamore. The smile meant
for me is cast, a shadow, past me. *Are you
happy?* I have asked her, asking her to lie.

AIRSTREAM

My mother's brother comes back one summer in five,
or one summer in seven, to what he does
not call his home. My mother does not blame
him, she claims; *there was nothing here for him.*
There was nothing here. She devils eggs.
She watches. *Mama rocked him till his feet*
dragged the floor, she tells me; *he was twelve years old*
when she died; he was just about your age.

He drives up at dusk, the swifts still spinning
in the last light. He pulls an old Airstream
behind him, and it glows, reflects the motion
of the sky, reflects my face, the faint moon.
I am called to crawl inside my uncle's
mirror, what he has brought from Oklahoma,
what he has brought from home. I have never
seen my mother cry she is so happy.

We are hours on the front porch; his boots
drag, drawl under the swing. The rust-chains
sing above his weight. He tells stories
about tornadoes: how he's seen a broomstraw
driven straight through a lightpole; he's seen a mirror
that was picked up and set back down unbroken
miles away; and once he saw a house
disappear except for a vase of fresh-cut flowers

that marked the plot like a grave. And he is not
afraid, has never been afraid of what
sends the natives down into their shelters
like prairie dogs. They think he's crazy not
to fear the sullen quiet of intense depression,
the horizon sick and jaundiced, the green lightning,
the buildings bursting from the higher pressure
that is trapped within them not unlike mean grief.

The wind comes unappeasable and coils
around itself, around the hollow core
of not-wind and crazed lightning; luminous
within its own dusk—dust-gorged and pulsing—
a hissing, ragged artery bleeds backwards
into itself; without edge, it spirals
what it did not choose of what was in its path,
all it keeps as futile, flawless memory

to be set down miles from home, in a rain of blood,
as the wind, still sinuous, dies again, again.
Imagine that, my mother says, *imagine*.
To her, he looks like one of us. He still
belongs, his forehead high, recognizable,
the way he laughs the same. I swing beside
him, terrified of all that he has seen.
I dream that night the wind flies me miles away

and sets me down so softly I cannot feel
myself. He wants to visit the old homeplace
and so we go with shovel and rake to repair
the graves that are all we own of that slow ruin.
Kudzu pulls the house down on itself
and poison ivy rises from the chimney.
Her grave has settled into a deepening
depression. *He was just about your age.*

He buries her again. Again he feels
that old fear not of any visible abyss
but of this furious, recurring worm—dust-gorged
and pulsing—and its slow, decomposing,
downward suck. What it takes into itself
is not set down except in memory—
what cannot be trusted—or in the slope
of a child's cheek, the angle of the brow—

all that the womb can mirror. He will have
his own wife and child, and less and less
of us. He will live his life where he
can see for miles. My mother cries all day
that day he leaves for home, the Airstream
luminous and rocking in a fog of dust
that picks up and swirls around itself, around
the sudden absence that has become the core.

ONE HAND ON THE WHEEL

Deep in the hot pine-needled shade
a 1940 model Plymouth rots like a roadside possum,
only slower, so slow the road's gone
rutless, grown up in trees and briars.
And like a living death the carcass blows out
toward scattered collapse; I find
severed doors flung far, and a bumper
grins in the leaves.
From the trunk sunk in the dirt to the headlights'
hollow sockets, rust worms away
roof and floorboard. Up through the driver's seat
a white sycamore struggles past the frame of windshield.
I trace it to the steering wheel the tree lifted out
like a soul; it rests loosely in the crook
of branch and body, where thumb meets hand,
lies smooth and fast against the lifeline.
Even as I admire such sure ascension,
what hope can I find in this reckless reclamation
when all else is an elbow out the window,
mindless of the road?

PORTRAIT

Twenty years' woodsmoke coats the glass
on her gilt-framed portrait,
but the pentimento's roving eye
catches his and is enough
and not even necessary
for him to see the night she cried
to die and he rubbed her back,
the liniment becoming
a molten membrane between his hands
and the bones rising
uprooted and disoriented
as if through still water.

He buried her under the red clover
while the cattle trudged closer,
heads low, chewing, puzzling.
Her milk cow's bell tolled:
This is where I am.

NOTHING FOR THE SALT

The cancer's in his bladder of all places.
If he has to have it, my father asks me, why
could it not be somewhere less shameful, if such
a place exists—a lung perhaps—something
to part the ribs for. They look into the depths
of him, he claims, as though for something sunken,
huge, irrecoverable. They've told him nothing
he doesn't know by now, his suspicion—
a persistent whisper in a dark house—proved.

He's been told what he can live without,
and he considers it, considers simply
getting up right now, leaving this room,
but he is tired, then suddenly comforted
by the supper tray and its long, cold arm's embrace.
He spoons his soup, commences an old story,
the past made new in its coincidence,
in this place where there's nothing—no fat, no salt, no sweet
to set his teeth around—to tell to me.

The day would come—pale, cold—a day well past
the lush declivity of summer. He tells
me on that day he'd hide inside the high,
black gape of the hayloft, where the poison

ivy climbed in to die, where the barn owl
brought the screaming rabbit, where he would later
find its fur and bones rendered neat and round—
mute and bloodless—would hold in the palm of his hand

the now imperfect memory of that scream
and be sure, suddenly, of nothing. He watched
the hog delivered from its pocked lot;
cupping his ears, heard anyway the distant

crack of the bullet to the brain. The rising,
blinding steam dispelled his father, blood
to his elbows, to whom he descended,
who handed him the one small joy of that day—

the severed bladder nothing to do with hog-piss,
nothing to do with hogs—more precious to him
than hams, hocks, shoulders. Nothing for the salt,
this thing made new in its divestment. When he held it,

he held the pale moon—inessential, but prized—
full of light and a father's breath—and setting
to rise above the smoke, above the scalding,
setting to rise again from the palm of his hand.

ABANDONED FARM GRAVE

How long since anyone visited here?
Your coffin has inhaled the earth.
Your tombstone has fallen facedown in the sinking.
I could heave over the stone and brush
your lost name, the date it was given you,
but that would not tell me where last
stories of you lie: in some newer grave,
closer to town, still visited, still mourned,
still another death away from you.

GOING ONCE, GOING TWICE

I.

The last aunt has died, my father's sister,
and now the rapturous auctioneer begins,
nods and weaves behind the microphone,
speaks in a tongue that we all understand
but cannot ourselves speak—a stuttered
eloquence to rival even the preacher
hired and touted to revive us all.
If we bid high enough, we will be saved.
He could hurl a poisonous serpent
into our midst, and we would welcome it.
We might then lay healing hands on the lame,
the sick, among us. My aunt could rise this soon
from the ineffectual dead. What would she choose
to keep if she walked with us amidst the strewing,
this inversion, the inside-out. Neighbors fingering
the chips in her good china, she, as well,
might move on past, deny us each in turn.

II.

My father bids and buys for next to nothing
the gourd he says they used to gather eggs;
he peers into its emptiness, tells me
he remembers growing it, its seed.
The cousins seek him out, call him to come
into the bottomless house where they've discovered
a shoebox filled with tintypes, portraits all
in black-and-white. His is, after all, the last
surviving memory for these who have
come this close to some ancestral abyss,
where graven, displaced names assume
again the latent image, are abstracted,
time-bound. He peers into the faces.
Over the rant of the auctioneer who pleads again,
again, *Are we all in and all done?*,

my father surprises us—and himself—as names
rise to his tongue, so long since they've been called
it is as if here, at the auctioned kitchen table,
he chooses them, christens the late: *Ruth, Maude, Julia-Kate.*

THE MILK COW SPEAKS OF WINTER

He pulls a full moon from my swollen bag;
the warm lunar landscape fogs far away
from me, though his forehead rises and falls
with each breath I take, light against my ribs.
Sometimes he speaks or sings or clucks his tongue,
and I watch him unfold his pocketknife,
sever the twine from another hay bale,
its dust rising with his icy white breath
as the tension collapses, relaxes
at his feet. I am offered last year's field,
and with the grass the rare brittle carcass
of a bird, grim beak hinged closed, the morning
glories smothered with their mouths wide open,
and the hollow bodies of grasshoppers
stunned midleap that morning he's forgotten.
He steals from the field as he steals from me.
I stand for him to curse and wrench the year's
staggering calf; at last I yearn to feel
his fists filling a galvanized bucket
with steady relief. And I lean into
his nuzzle, silent, my tongue the thick wind
that rolls over his chapped winter field,
my teeth sweet with red blossoms of clover.

II

THE MOON IS MADE

Phil sold cigarettes and soft drinks up front
and poured peach brandy in the back room
of his corner gas station. Summers,
my brother and I would ride our bikes
around the two pumps to ring the bell,
and Phil would yell not to and not mean it.
He sliced rat cheese from a huge wheel, waned
by appetite like a foul yellow moon
flat on its back; in deep July heat
it reeked its gravitational pull.
We bought hunks in white butcher paper
and Saltines for lunch; hunkered down
inside on cool concrete, we listened
to Phil talk dirty about women.
Well, you think, that's all a fine memory,
except that even though I tried to
hide it with high tops and a Cubs cap,
I was a little girl, and I knew
he knew it. But even my big brother
only laughed when Phil rolled back the tin
on kippers and said, "Don't let your nose
stop your tongue every time." And he winked
at me, at what he knew I would be,
then tossed back his head, dropped a headless
fish in his mouth to swim blindly down
while my shame, nameless, soured and curdled,
and the moon fumed and overcame me.

IN THE ACOUSTIC SHADOW

I think she liked to frighten me with it.
The great-aunt held the minié ball in her palm,
a small egg, bone-gray lead, and said, "This is
The Wilderness. This is how close you came
to that common Confederate grave."
I never tired of it or the story
of how this improbable artifact lodged
sixty years in the trench it had burrowed
in her grandfather's temple; how his skull
closed over it easy as a tree heals
around barbed wire, scarred but defiant,
defined not by deformity but pain;
how to remove it would have killed him; how
he feared sharing the grave with it and made
her grandmother swear to have it cut from
his dead body and she did, as if that
could deliver him too late from memory;
how the story of who shot him was told
by its three-ringed base: *a Yankee, at least
it was a Yankee*; how folks passed around
what did not kill him—this dormant tumor;
how it came to rest in her grandmother's
jewelry box, sunk beneath the cameos
and brooches; how the heirloom came to be
hers.
        "This is The Wilderness," she told me,
and I believed her, believed the battle
unburied raged on, and I believed I stood
this close, pale in the acoustic shadow,
my disconception safe in her palm.

ROMANTIC FEVER

I fought the lost summer of '58
from the narrow sun-porch bed; rheumatic
fever clenched a fist in every joint.
My skin seared white-hot sheets my mother washed
every day and hung on the line like sails
swollen pointlessly against anything
anchored this deep. She plugged in the Zenith
for me; rock and roll melted in morphine.
Jerry Lee's new release, "Great Balls of Fire,"
played every hour to unborn irony.

By September, pale legs like pain-hollowed
stems and wrists as weak as oak leaves', I was
fragile but redeemed, capable of growth,
sent to school where I swayed by the lockers,
watched as the viral rumor caught and spread:
She's been in bed with romantic fever.

That night I lay harbored in the darkness,
watching the doomed fireflies rise; easier
to believe the stars had fallen, crippling
in the trees. In the damp grass one lay flat
on its back, coughing up light.

SKIN DEEP

I can still feel his hard, sharp knees beneath
my bony rump, but I can recall no
stories until the great-aunt gives me his
trunk, its hollow back as humped as his was.
In it, a mouse's long-deserted nest
covers shirt collars still starched; his razor;
strop; shaving brush; fogged tintypes of strangers;
and her brittle love-letters, bound in red
ribbon, their addresses fine blue, bloodless
as the dispassionate cursive on the backs
of her hands; and beneath the letters
his Waterman fountain pen, its lung collapsed.
In the bottom of the trunk, like something
forgotten, long-treasured, or completely
incidental to him, lies the shed
skin of a snake; when I lift it, it rasps,
fragile, transparent, and empty:

One still August night when I was twelve and my three cousins not
much older,
We left the curing barns and slipped away to go skinny-dipping in
Bearskin Creek.
We had a lantern and a stingy half-moon between us; I could barely
make out the white mule
Fog-hobbled on the cooling banks, where we stooped down to untie the
laces of our shoes,
Where I heard again, then again, the sound of fists on the water, and I
whispered, "Wait, boys, wait,"
And swung up the lantern to make out one, then two, then a slew of
them draped in low branches
Against the moon, and their writhing dives to no more evil purpose
than boys who have
Worked too long as men, to no more temptation than not to belly, but
fly blind
Down the sweeter currents of one cooler night. We surrendered it to
them

And scrambled back to the hot, infernal crop we had been determined to
*   save.*

I lay the snakeskin back where I found it,
fingering its scaled seamlessness to the mute
mouth that has opened wide and released the head
like a tongue, and on that tongue all sense, all
poison, an essential voice telling
itself from its nest of dispossessions.

BEDTIME STORY

Sometimes I can believe it was a dream,
but it is only memory, even old
memory that perverts itself so, adorns
itself with dissolution and all
the bad translation truth can stand. Listen
to it and learn to sleep when you are told,
and if you wake screaming from a nightmare
real enough to drag me upstairs to you,
stay in bed, hear me, keep your eyes closed:

*All the high windows raised to a black heat; they had no screens in those
   days,*
*And the fireflies burned against the ceiling. She was unaccustomed to late
   guests, and this much laughter,*
*Perfume, and sweet smoke drew her to the stairwell. She looked down on
   flame and falling wax,*
*And her mother's best tablecloth waved with shadow as if in a wind. They
   threw back their heads,*
*Their mouths blooming like hot orchids, and drank what was dark as
   honey and stained the linen.*
*In front of her father—it must have been her father because he always
   carved—*
*Was a ribcage, a chest no broader than hers—flayed, gutted, stuffed, flayed
   and gutted again,*
*And she held her hand to her mouth; the fingers the calf sucked could feel
   again the sudden*
*Hot pull to her palm, his breath spice-sweet, his tongue fattened for quiet.
   She watched the wild plums,*
*Soaked a year in brandy, passed around the table; plucked from their scald-
   ing syrup, they scorched*
*The tongues of guests who pulled out the inedible stones like thorns and
   cast them one by one*
Through the high window as if seeding the heat.
                              *Every spring thereafter
   the bees would murmur truth*
*While her mother explained that crows came, planted, and with black strut
   tamped the soil,*

That calves were sold and grown as prize seed-bulls who pawed the
    ground with missing her,
And that hounds growled over a windfall of moon-shards, pocked and cold.
    Good for cutting
Teeth, but shy of meat.

      Get your thumb out of your mouth and go to sleep.

PRODIGAL

This road is deep now as a riverbed,
mud-packed under a dry, sometime current
of balding tires and hooves. I know if I
had stayed, this new depth would be imperceptible.
My father stands at the end of it, an old
man now, ruts and gullies washed in his face.
Before he can speak, a peacock screams, opens
its blind, repeating eye, and fans me with
a familiar mask. "He is the last of them,"
my father says, "he struts for doves, crows,
the wind." The house behind him lists toward
ruin, toward mistletoe clots in the oak-rot;
on the roof a skew of rods, their green-glass eyes
beg lightning.
                        "Come on," he says and moves into
and through the stable-gloom. By the rotting harness
and rust-bit I am sure the mare is dead,
but he says not—moon-blind, old, but there—
and points to her, grazing black against
the barbed horizon, beside a thin spring calf.
He's in the middle of tearing down the tractor—
slain, dismembered. An oily ligature
seeps into the ground. "I know I ought
to buy a new one, but I won't," he tells me
as if I don't know he doesn't take well to failure.
"Let's go get us up a supper," he says,
and we walk to the garden's blank plot, but when
he pulls from the ground a ruddy beet, I see
he's planted a crop of roots: turnips, sweet
potatoes grown the color of his hands.
"You don't need teeth for such as these," he laughs,
and moves away from me as if I am
forgiven. I lose my taste for this late
feast; I lose my breath. But there at the edge
of the woods the mushrooms, wild, breathe for me
through dusky gills, and I succumb, follow
him, my fists root-bound and rich with blood.

FORTUNE

When she complains of a splinter, his own
tired illness is for that moment lost as he
holds her hand in his, peers into her
palm as if to read it, translate the line
of fate, measure her life, deny deceit
in her at all. He keeps his eye on the splinter
as he unfolds the blade of his pocketknife,
honed to within a sliver of its life

but still holding its edge from all the years
of spit and stone on steel. She looks from him
into some painless distance, does not flinch,
is still waiting when he at last breathes, *there,*
and folds again the blade that, like keen marrow,
anticipates the necessary bone.

PLAGUES

A rain crow lusts in the hot, waxy pines.
Day after day a red-tail thirsts against
the flat sky: the field mice dry and dying,
there is nothing worth leaving the thermals.
Tobacco burns in the fields, and corn
smothers in its silk. The cows, blowsy, slow,
brood in the sallow pond, hooves sunk, sucking
silky mud that rises like blood.
                                        "Smitten,
we are smitten with old plagues." The great-aunt
waves her hands, her thin forearms sumac-red
with easy bruises.
                        "Aw, listen to you,"
I humor her, "we are having a drought,
but the almanac—"
                        "—did not predict these
seventeen-year locusts." She's mad now. "'Pharaoh,
Pharaoh,' hear them plead?"
                                I listen, but hear
wordless their persistent rumor. "I don't know
about that, Aunt Kate; I don't remember
the Bible like you do."
                        "I would tear out
your tongue like a bloody root," she tells me,
"but I am tired," lays down her head in her
narrow lap. A hymn trembles, rises from
her thighs: *Shall we gather at the river?*

The neighbor cranks the '49 Ford motor
that runs his irrigation pump, faithless:
the fields shoulder the rank beat of wings, wings
of bitter water. All night the orphaned
locusts wheeze in the darkness, grafted now
with disinherited language, until
we are all of one mind, one swollen tongue:
Pharaoh, Pharaoh, as if there were something
keeping us, as if we could be let go.

FIRST TOOTH

Every night, beside the bed, her bared teeth—
false, flawless—hung in water, suspended,
like what she pickled—an egg or a beet, the feet of a pig—
or something fetal, incomplete—what I had seen
through glass and formaldehyde at the fair: the twins
joined by one coincident spine, their eyes
closed, the two umbilical cords still trailing

off, lost thoughts, in opposite directions.
That night the same, Grandmother read the Bible aloud,
her words gone soft; from her blunted tongue, vowels poured
like oil. With my tongue I worried the loose tooth,
rocking it looser in its socket until I tasted
blood. I heard *Your teeth are like a flock*
of shorn ewes that have come up from the washing,

all of which bear twins, and not one among them
is bereaved. My tooth, a white seed, I would plant
beneath my pillow, and it would bear another
self in the place it lost. I did believe
what she told me, that I could bleed without
dying, and I opened my mouth, let her choke
the root with her scarlet sewing thread, and pull.

III

BAIT

I won't take the metaphoric leap,
won't leave this splintered dock
with all its illusion of land; I can ignore
the temperamental sun casting and reeling in
your shadow across the water.

But when you slide the earthworm like a stocking
over the sharp toe, the smooth curve
of this wicked, hooked leg, tell me again how
the bloodless vessel feels no pain as you pierce
the first of its abundant hearts.

BAIT MAN

I was spawned in lost waters. We all were,
but because I can no longer walk, because
this stillness halves me now, I know to hate
why a bass pauses, hovers in still water,
slime-thick and foul, beneath a rotted log.
He is safe, he thinks, at a great distance
from death, though it is death that feeds him, casts
its bait—dull worm and black, panicked beetle—
from the punk of the log, the same as I cast mine.
I, too, struck at what drifted in the womb.

I. Before

The wide, bloodless mouth closes around
the promise and its lie. Some of us learn
to breathe again. I washed my granny's feet,
her tongue—fluent and strange—flying in her mouth.
The preacher lunged, pulled from behind her ear
the cancer like a coin and hurled it down,
ground it with his heel into the dust.
I was saved in that clear water where I held
my breath, opened my eyes to white robes rising
and fishes, damned, drifting in the folds.

I was always drawn to what I could
not see. But I could feel the draw of the worm's
cold bloat in muck—the moment of conception
when the cord is sunk in the belly. Water breaks
to a bass flying, his body lost to old,
familiar motion. Long into the waning
afternoon, I would wade waist-deep
in all he knew, casting and recasting,
and feel him move against me in the creel—
a backward womb—as if he died inside me.

Before the accident, I painted roofs:
mansard, gable, shed, and hip. Bound burning

waist to cross, I have painted many
a church steeple, the pigeons circling beneath me.
In summer, silver paint would blind. I've seen
above the moon-bored fog a barn roof shine
above no barn—disembodied—hover
like a weightless plane, some new heavenly
body, filled with stolen light that holds
as I did to that pitch, but does not fall.

II. The fall

I know the dream is nothing but a scar,
healed and pale and nothing like the wound;
still, I live for sleep, for that willful leap
into recurrence. My shirt swells, and I rise,
raptured by the slur of the wind. Below me
in the broom sedge, a crow lies on its belly—a pupil
shrunken, sunk in its deep, bronze iris.
The breeze teases a black feather; the quill
lifts, flesh-bound but light. The field, blind,
redefines itself, stares backwards, past me.

You have to ask how does it feel? How does it
feel? April seining, waist-deep in cold so
cold you stand waist-deep in nothing, the net
writhing and heavy, wrestling you down. Or frozen
in hot light, you are gigged; your legs—severed
from you without being severed—suddenly
jump as if on hot iron, your thighs sere-white.
You are your own trophy; you have survived
your own death, your head hung on the wall
that keeps you from the feast that was yourself.

You think you would bear easier a bullet
in your spine, some dark fragment, a deep,
unreachable fault lodged there like an axis,
a new equator x-rayed and charted—the point

from which you sail into some other world,
the point from which you are turned back, your legs
ignorant, vain as heavy, braided hair.
You would bear easier an enemy to hate,
and gravity is faceless. And water,
bearing a still face, still won't be walked on.

III. After

To make this living, I sell line and hooks,
lures and lies. Mainly I sell bait:
nightcrawlers and worms—whatever bellies and wears
a hook well—and crickets, black and pale,
massed in a box that stinks of rot and writhing.
They do not use their legs for singing; they are
too desperate, I guess, too crowded. The minnows
complain the same way. Though I am good to them
and change the water in their tank, they still
refuse and leap from it sometimes to deeper

water that is not there. They leap instead
to deepest air, where the current is light
and won't float them. If I see them fly,
I pick up, one by one, the arcing bodies,
then open my fist to release them in the tank.
If water's what they want, then I am glad,
but if they hesitate, I cast them out
to what they must desire. Death fouls the water
and won't make bait. A bass strikes best at what swims
as if delighted with the hook in its back.

In my time, I have cleaned a multitude
like this. In a fish's belly I have found
the smaller fish, the ragged hook, and once
a brassy ring. I have opened a bass
like a book to its fine-sewn spine and seen myself
in the worm that withers. A reluctant prophet,

I was swallowed up to breathe these days
underwater, where I miss the feel of my heels
beneath me, where I am patient not to die
but to be vomited at last, whole, upon the shore.

THE TAXIDERMIST

In good weather I herd them onto my lawn,
coats glossy, feathers bold. Cars slow for the fox
beside the quail, the bobcat by the sleeping
fawn. I turned each body inside out,
emptied it of flesh, fat, bones, eyes; the meat
of the lie displays the thin, defining skin
of something else. All that you see, I save.
Good enough to shoot again, you laugh,
but I know death is not held at bay, has not
even looked over its shoulder at the fleshing knives
and pliers, the saws and scalpels. This is tedious,
messy resurrection, and what I preserve
is not death or life or skill but the wounded
ghost of an old hunger that won't be tamed
and taught to lick your hand, old hunter, but will
bound through some finer field, beyond the wind
you foul, even as I rummage for the right
glass eye in drawered compartments. Here, see,
they are all here: loon, lynx, buck, fox, quail,
snake, and coon. All measured, all perfect, all blind.

TIMEPIECE

He laughed and said you can keep time, but time
will not be kept. He bent before my watch,
its back open to its still, distemporal gut.
All about him, clocks stood or lay—gaining, losing,
dismembered, dead. At best, they disagreed,
struck the hour for half an hour, a cuckoo last
with a pained, consumptive wheeze. He passed his days
peering through a glass magnifying what
cannot be seen, knowing well the nothing paused
when he paused the pendulum and held it
pulseless.
            The story has it he was lowered
down into a well to repair the wall,
falling down the depth of itself. He was
lowered to restore the tension, all that
keeps a wall from its deepest longing.
The sky hung like a shrunken sun, the sun
itself now lost to him. He swung above
the water, was just midway between it
and his last deep breath when the wall fell— a bone
closing down around its own strange marrow—
claiming him as it would have claimed the void
that had hung there for all the years before him.

There is a terrible space between the past
and all prediction, between the origin
and its last descent. And in that space he found
there is light, and the reflection of light, but darkness
and its reflection are one. As a snake holds
in its belly the egg—in its insistent shell—
he was held those days, the story has it,
while men removed, stone by stone, what kept him,
hour by hour. He must have dreamed the windless water
rose—sweet and clean—bringing up the dark-carved moon,
bringing up the sky, that he might drown in it.

Without the balanced falling weight and hands
like the hands of the blind on a stranger's face, without
the absolute agreement with the sun,
shadowless, that makes this noon, we are
lost to a middling-now at once narrow
and infinite;
                    a clock stopped is right
twice a day, he said, and that is failure;
is its frozen soul lodged in the blood, the marrow,
the brain? —in deep, past the last bone, lies the stubborn
muscle, the one spring wound to release its spiraled tension.

His cheek against that feverish stone, he found
what he would now deny, that time would not
be measured, that it was wholly ignorant
of the blood that pulsed in him, ignorant
of the redundant sun and its essential
rising. He was at last raised up to August
heat and the crazed, voiceless screaming of the locusts,
a dove's condolent, hollow call. He breathed
and watched a wasp drone by, its legs dangling
as if broken in the air beneath it. The wall
lay undone all about the bloodied mouth
of the well. The story has it he was never
the same. He took a liking to these finer,
delicate tasks.
                    He placed again the back
on my watch, its resurrected *tick.* All
about us, the hour was told and retold—joyous,
doleful, as if fact. He told me this was twelve
o'clock and set the hands for me. He held
the face to his ear and heard what he said was hard
for him to hear, it was so akin to silence.
Then, from the farthest corner of the room,
again the cuckoo roused itself and—not
unlike the original bird—sang out this noon,
or, being blinded, told this brighter midnight.

IV

TRANSGRESSIONS

I.

He sat in the open doorway. Closed, blank
as any door, he looked at me, and the years
between us distilled down to familiar
disappointment: a pointed, trembling finger,
a raised eyebrow the one loose plank in his face.
A crow panted as if breathless, let down
its sun-white wings; sleeping in the trees
the guineas shimmered like heavy, restless fruit;
a grackle looked past us, its white eye doubtful,
bored with what it had already seen;
and the swamp oak, uprooted by forgotten ice,
leafed out against the ground—a fallen sky—
insistent, too, that all was as before.
On the porch, his old hound lay belly-up,
asleep, and he pulled from behind its ear
a tick—an imperfect pearl, blood-fat—
and considered it before he cast it down
and spoke to me. He knew I was the one
come home to help him stay here, die here, to wish him
dead, to suffer this, my own survival.
And he saw me as his Judas, ordained,
a necessary betrayal; though there would be
no final kiss to mark it, the question was
the selfsame lie because the answer—then
as now unspoken—was known: *Why are you here?*

II.

I was mowing the hay, and the field that had been wind
in hay and braided morning glories lay flat,
dying. I had forgotten how quail panic
before the sickle bar, how a fawn mangles
and still won't move, how a buzzard, having forgotten
nothing, circles—patient for the flesh
strewn with the grain—how even crows' rejoicing

45

sounds like despair, might be despair that this is
what there is.
             I found him slumped over
himself, his left side dead, and I held him
in my arms and prayed—the prayer still sour
in my mouth—for his breath to leave him still as that
breathless noon. But the crows' wings beat against
the sun, against his face, and his chest fell
to rise, measuring the difference
between what was asked and what was given.

III.

He thumped his arm against the arm of his chair—
a sound like knocking snow off wet firewood.
But this bruised, bled like a living thing—
felt nothing. He considered what must be
his own pain as if from a great distance,
then looked at me; my being here was proof
he was alive. I learned his body, bathed him—
withered gut and groin—washed his hands, his face,
his back, his thighs.
             He told me what he wanted,
his tongue so thick it was another language
we both learned, the words foreign, broad,
familiar as a dream remembered late
in the morning. *Here, come here* like slow oil flowed from his
    mouth.

IV.

Then in the evenings we sat on the porch to watch
night fall at last from dusk, and he would rhyme
a whippoorwill with a slower, hollow call,
close enough so it would come up—sometimes
close enough for us to see its moon-cast
shadow—forgiving him everything for the lust
in the voice that called from our shared darkness.

BARN CAT

I have heard the talk, how she—accused
of suicide by what she refused—let go
this place and herself. Now we're all here
to divide among us what she has not
already willed away—what mattered most,
or not at all: the sunken house, the brace
of swayed mules, querulous hens, the outbuildings
skeletal, wind-scoured.
                    Though her root cellar is empty,
the stable still groans, magnificent with hay;
from under it, one of the barn cats, nameless,
staggers and stands. I can see it's been days
dying and isn't done yet: a maggot-burned
dissection bares hipbone, living sinew;
the shank moves with flies. This is no wound, this
rude decay. I know I could go to her
house and find loaded, still leaning behind her
kitchen door, the single-shot .22
and with mercy kill what has refused the place
where animals go to die, kill what has risen
out of resolve, inspired, and moves toward me,
as if toward death, who will not despair
to save her, will not mistake this sudden taming.

MORPHINE DREAMS

Pain casts a waning shadow here. It moves,
dark and cool, as the shade of a tree moves,
winds through me until I fall past sleep,
past dream, past what time my grown sons—awkward,
already dressed for the wake—will wait for me.
I fall away from what has conceived itself
in me; like light from a swollen moon, I fall
from what has gorged itself on all I was.
Ravenous for air, it opens my mouth
so it can breathe. But I am past it now.
The needle,

         quick, moves over and under.
I can make it look so easy, boneless
as an otter, wet and sharp as it dives and rises.
The blind eye pulls the thread. The pocked thimble
ticks hard as bone. The baby kicks, but I
am seamless. See, I slip my hand under
the belly of the hen and steal from her
I am so smooth; I am seamless as her egg,
boneless; I beat the whites with a fork until
they lighten like the down in my pillow.
He talks with his mouth full of that down; he says
the field is sown and laughs and pats my belly,
swallows me whole I am so light and boneless.
I am all tongue, thick as a calf's; wordless,
it is thick with milk and holds like an egg one vowel
seamless and whole. I hold the field in my mouth,
the field blue with chicory, blue with wind
coursing through it. I am lost in the maze of my own
veins. I bruise, bleed deep and clean; see how
white the sheet the needle plunges, quick,
moves over and under; the pocked thimble
ticks hard as bone. I can make it look easy,
bloodless. I will bear Sleep his weary son,
who will lie on my shoulder, turn his head—
slow and sweet—against me, wake, and leave me light.

STABLE

One rusty horseshoe hangs on a nail
above the door, still losing its luck,
and a work-collar swings, an empty
old noose. The silence waits, wild to be
broken by hoofbeat and heavy
harness slap, will founder but remain;
while outside, above the stable,
eight, nine, now ten buzzards swing low
in lazy loops, a loose black warp
of patience, bearing the blank sky
like a pall of wind on mourning
wings. But the bones of this place are
long picked clean. Only the hayrake's
ribs still rise from the rampant grasses.

GOSSIP

They say I outlived him. With me, they watched
him waste, his muscle fall from him, his bones
rise into the sheet. They saw him laid out,
sent under where there is no worm deep enough
for what still sleeps with me, for that sourceless,
dry skittering in the walls: every night
I still rise into what he called morning;
every morning I drink buttermilk
that was before too thick, too heavy
on my tongue. It took me years to learn
to live with it. Now, what would I drink? When
would I rise? They come visit and talk,
and patient for my story, they tell me
theirs: the high blood, the nerves—mysterious, thrumming
nerves—the sugar, the stillborn and breech birth,
the fallen womb, or—the size of some sweet
fruit—the deep, inoperable tumor.

The horse he had when we married would not
be worked or ridden or harnessed. There were no
rearing hysterics: only the whip
fluent in the air, only a shudder
in the traces—the quiet madness
of refusal. Proud he didn't kill it,
he said many a man would have. It stood
years in the stable. There was no chinking
between the logs, and when the light was right,
I could make out its broken silhouette.
One winter night, I saw it out grazing ice,
its breath the smoke of a dead fire. Beyond it,
the fence swayed, the field gaped as if bewildered
at that brute inability to see
freedom as distance. I despised it,
was glad when it died and he dragged its body
out and burned it. A still day, the smoke rose
and would not leave the pasture.
                                    There is nothing to tell past

the small bone, sunk in the meat, that lodges
in the throat deeper than pulse, blood, breath, voice.
I have a photograph of our golden
wedding anniversary: we hold the knife,
stainless, over a white cake. I mourn
a photograph of his corpse. Lies, all lies.
Airless as mud, the field still chinks the dark
stall. The wagon's tongue is driven in the dust.

STOIC

He has brought again the dozen fall calves;
they bawl and slide from the cattle-hauler,
but she knows by dusk they'll have found their path
prescribed along the fenceline. By morning
rain will have washed the shit from them, and clean
as from afterbirth, they will travel
the spiraled pasture; stoic, they will learn
to read the sky and know what kneeling down
can save. She sees one has a white heart
figured on its forehead; all carry black
markings on their bodies as if continents
were mapped here, and the charted unknown steams,
shudders, on its ribbed shelf, unnavigable.
Better known, the doe-goat he stakes closer,
then farther; her rope, taut as a compass
needle, sweeps toward the magnetic elsewhere
that lies beyond gnomon fenceposts, beyond
the grid of windrows, beyond the distance
that holds her in coincidence. The scythe
swings against the stable wall, bears the arc
of some skeletal sextant, horizon-dulled,
mirrorless, useless in this rain-fat grass.
She can—she tells him over heavy-laden
supper platters—tell one calf from the others,
but she hears her voice rise with the steam
past its leaving, dissipate into silence,
as the meat, complacent, falls from the bone.

LOOKING FOR GRANDMOTHER'S GRAVE

This landscape is his familiar: clocks stopped,
the women shrouding her body, the wake,
her coffin in the rude wagon, her grave
in the cedar grove beyond the field where
tobacco stood half-pulled and top-heavy.

"I know durn well she's here somewhere."
My father disremembers this changeling
acreage of sixty-foot loblollies
in worn furrows, deeded and redeeded: his
disinheritance. Somewhere they are here,
plow-scars the letters only he can read.
Not alone that day in swearing he'd pay
for her name in marble, he tells me shame
kept him away from the mound of fieldstones
that mark her grave. Now fifty years later
he's the first to return, can't find a single
cedar, says to watch the ground for a bed
of periwinkle: grave flowers. But I
see thistle and foxglove seed this ground;
their suggestions take in the still-poor soil.
My father's legs are covered now in burrs,
beggar-lice.
        Her bones are swaddled in tree roots,
I think, *nameless.* "At least I know this much,"
I say, "I could come this close."
                        Disconsolation,
I hear too late. Suddenly, my father
ventures: "A hawk," never looking up, eyes
firmly on the ground. I search the sun, am
blinded trying, but cannot see what casts
the shadow that staggers and falls between us.

HAWK

A deer scut rocks away
from the road's white ellipses.
Fish rise, slow in the still pond.
Smoke falls from the chimney's mouth
as you, always at your window,
watch your sunflower seed draw songbirds:
small worries squabble, flutter in and out.

My shadow flags the clean spires of trees,
freezes in the garden a rabbit
who does not trust what blocks the sun,
but what you enjoy is this
span of wings, their rare, calm beat,
my tail a red fan open, you think, to catch
the sun, complement the sky.

Look away or watch: hunger
for your songbird that flies no higher than roses climb
will lift it from its precious nest,
deliver it of its cooling eggs. Even as it dies,
even as it climbs these deeper currents
with me, even as you see in this what you need
and try even now to love me, listen:

These wings are not my wings.
These bones are not my bones;
I spit them out.
This song is not my song,
mine this denial,
unmeasured, unsung; I hurl it,
unfeathered and bone-hollowed, down.

PHOENIX

for CCG

The *whys* are all supposed and of a kind:
lost love, what she fought in the mirror, the change of life.
Perhaps there was no one thing that nestled her finger,
neat, against the trigger, that drove the bullet
in the brain, that mussed at last the hair she'd worn
the same way since 1963.
                                    We pray
over an urn—even her ashes clean, contained.
She would, by request, cheat the slower worm.
Still, I fear for her what does not burn, and hope
at least she left this place—if self indeed
proved inescapable—the way she would
have left in 1964—behind
the wheel, say, of a Galaxy, a Fury,
a Thunderbird—some long, fast car
on a road writhing in light shed like slow skin
from a perfect moon. Flying, flying, she is
swaddled in white, the ragtop down, her head
thrown back; the wind—fine in her hair—begins
to burn. But she only laughs, floors it, will be gone before
this fire consumes itself in the void from which she rises.

INHERITANCE

They served me cider in their darkened parlor
and tarts beneath a stiff meringue. The great-aunts,
old and childless, had always looked, wistfully
relieved, on me with love. I knew I would
inherit what little there was: this thinning, brittle
cup I balanced trembling on my knee,
the brooch I thought I'd never wear at the base
of my throat. I breathed their cloved breath and steadied
myself for the way it was—those old, hard times
the only time worth telling this often and with this
much love, because they had indeed survived what
the one sister, my grandmother—the myth—had not.
Again, the great-aunts told me that where I came from

> whatever bird a man had brought home dead
> a woman used from brain to claw. A man
> might think as far as sweet breast meat, but she
> would look to finer things, would fashion herself
> a fan from a wing, and fan herself in the hot
> church-house, fan her breast and soul against
> the thick and rising heat. And she was not
> alone in this. The sanctuary moved
> with a sluggish beat; what bore up flesh and breath
> would fly wild against stained windowpanes, against
> that much framed sky—if it could escape her.

The great-aunts told me they were all the temptation
to immortality there was, and the preacher worked himself
into a palsied dream for them, saying

> *Let your tongue rise from its vileness wild*
> *like Lazarus rise from the stinking cave*
> *of your mouth. Let your tongue speak what has*
> *not been spoken it has been so long*
> *dead. The apple tree bears its awful*
> *fruit—as you do sister—and the taste*
> *of the fruit is the same even as the fruit*
> *is not the same. Only the worm*

moves unchanged through it and will
find your flesh on its dark tongue sweeter
than any apple's. Even the hornet
falls drunk on the fallen fruit and staggers
through the air, will fall into the fire,
its belly filled with flesh gone hard
not as hard as your flesh, sister,
not as hard as your heart rotting
there beneath your flowering breath,
there beneath your breast, yes, there.

And the sisters bound their breasts and wound their hair
and opened their mouths in thanksgiving for him to
    place
the host there: *This is my body:*
                            The guttural
muscle of the fall calf's tongue lay fat and dumb
on my grandmother's tongue. Her mouth closed slow
    around
a milk-suckled silence. She ate all of it.
With the butt of her knife, she cracked the baked hen's
    skull
like an egg, dug out the delicate brain, this above
the clutter of tattered bones—back, wing, and thigh.

The wild meat darker, leaner—gamey. She
could close her eyes and taste the sassafras leaves,
the apples hard and cidery, the evening dew.
If she could hold the night on her tongue, it would taste
like this doe who had swung as a suicide swings,
suspended above the rest of us, her belly
opened and divested of all that had defined her:
lung, hunger, heart, desire, the slow compulsion
of blood. She did dream night, gutted, tasted
like this—at once dead, and so deliciously wild.

Sunk deep in the featherbed, she did return
to water—conceived and labored, bore quick and dead.

In the eaves and in the wall a hive would hum
in summer heat, hum all night every night,
a thousand, thousand wings fanning, keeping
cool the queen—that one dark, fertile thought,
sunk deep in the folds—that had for months eaten
the sweet, bright fields and grown fat with envy of
    flight.

The great-aunts nodded; in their dream their napkins
fluttered to the floor. The sisters saw me then
to the door, their brittle lips trembling
sweet against my lips, against my cheek,
as if in betrayal. Outside, butterflies,
dying, staggered through those last mild days.
A jackhornet, already drunk and mean,
had laid its eggs underground, and now
before me carried for the larvae to eat in the spring
a locust. The sting I knew had cast it deep
into a sleep for which there was no kiss
sweet enough to waken lucent wings
that would forever shroud the body. Blind
and rutting, I, too, had cut my teeth on what
had long ago been left me, on what had not
died, but would, in time, outlive its season.

And to her, I owe this terrible desire
for lightness, a dark longing to wake to crow-
black wings, to hold in my mouth not some sweet
insistent lyric—but the one raucous thought that bears
repeating, to carry between my lips the wild
plum—round as a vowel—become perfect, singular
in its loss of the world, to steal away from here
the vain detail I love—a thing bright and shiny
that bears its saving: a thimble, a ring, a needle—
its only eye worn wide, diminishing.